MW01245838

IMMANUEL

25 DAYS OF DEVOTIONS FOR CHRISTMAS/ADVENT

BY ANDY BLANKS

PUBLISHED BY YM360

ABOUT THIS BOOK

Do you know what the phrase, "a sense of wonder" means? To have a sense of wonder is to possess a deep curiosity about things, to be able to still be surprised about certain aspects of the world around you. Having a sense of wonder means not being so used to the world around you that you stop thinking about it as a really awesome place.

Do you still notice amazing sunsets?
Are you still blown away by the concept of outer space? Galaxies? Universes? Stars?
Do you ever step back and think about how cool it is that we can have complex, meaningful relationships with other humans?

If you have a sense of wonder, these are things you do on a regular basis.

One of the most unfortunate truths about our lives is that we are quick to lose our sense of wonder. This is true about how we interact with everything from nature to technology. This is especially true about matters of faith.

The overwhelming majority of you reading this have heard the Christmas story so many times that maybe you have lost your sense of wonder for it.

Let's change that this Christmas.

Immanuel means "God with us." That's what Jesus was: God with us. The Christmas story is arguably the most, wonder-inspiring story ever told. It's the story of God becoming human in the form of a little, defenseless baby. It was an important chapter in the story of God's desire to rescue humanity from the penalties of sin. And yet, sometimes we are guilty of letting Christmas move right past us without stopping to just soak up the WONDER of it all.

Let this book be your guide to re-discovering the wonder for God and His amazing story to save us, His children. Don't lose your sense of wonder this Christmas. Instead, nurture it. Open your eyes to what God did and let Christmas become a launching pad to a deeper relationship with Jesus, our *Immanuel.*

DAY 1 ISAIAH 9:6-7

There are those passages in the Bible that we seem to hear a lot at Christmas. Isaiah 9:6-7 is one of them. Take a moment and read these verses. Because we've listened to them so often, these are probably pretty familiar. Because of this, we can easily kind of pass over its importance. But don't let it slip past you this time.

Isaiah 9:6-7 was written by Isaiah, arguably the greatest prophet of Israel. Isaiah was passing along God's words at a time when God's chosen people had turned their backs on God and had stopped counting on God and His promises. Because of this, and after a lot of warning by God, Isaiah's message warned the Israelites of the judgment that was coming their way. But because God's love is unfailing, even His message of judgment carried hope.

Isaiah 9:6-7 is all about a future in which God once and for all provides a way out from under the weight of our sins. Fast forward something like 700-800 years and you see this message of hope coming to life in the Christmas story. The baby God was forming in Mary's stomach? He was the same promised savior Isaiah was writing about in Isaiah 9:6-7.

If you want to nurture your sense of wonder, take a moment and let this awesome truth sink in. Long before God sent Jesus to this earth, He knew the plan. God's sending His own Son to live and breathe and walk this earth was always the plan. God has always known that Jesus would be the answer to a perfect relationship between God and His children, which is excellent news for you and me. But to see this plan come to life, Jesus had to come to earth. Immanuel! And that's what Christmas is all about.

CONSIDER THIS . . .

• If you have a saving faith relationship with Jesus, the future God has in store for you is full of hope. How does that help you trust Him with your worries, concerns, and future?

• Take a moment to pray to God, thanking Him for being a God who loves us enough to send His Son to live among us to ultimately save us.

DAY 2 MATTHEW 1:1-17

Take a moment and read Matthew 1:1-17. What a list of names! (SO many names.) Some of them are kind of weird, some of them are relatively normal, but all of them are important. You probably recognize some of them from familiar Bible stories. (Hopefully, you identified at least a few.) But what's the big deal about this list of names?

This list isn't just some strange, random piece of info that would have been important for the Bible's original audience. This list is important for a few reasons. First, it proves that Jesus is the promised Messiah. According to the Old Testament, the Messiah was to be God's ruler, who would one day be sent to restore the Israelites. (Of course, we know that Jesus did more than save the Israelites; through His death and resurrection, Jesus provided a way for all who will believe in Him to be saved from their sins.) Old Testament prophecy said that the Messiah would come from the line of David. Look back at verse 7. Whose name do you see?

This list actually contains a lot of really cool stories, way more than we have time to go into in this devotion. But the important thing about this list is that, for Matthew's original audience, it provided some validity, or authenticity for Jesus' claim that He was indeed the Messiah.

Jesus, God with us, was who He said He was. His life attested to it. His death and resurrection confirmed it. And it all started with His birth.

CONSIDER THIS . . .

• Where do you see examples of the world around you doubting Jesus as the Son of God?

• How does reading the Bible and praying to God help you trust that He is real and that He loves you?

• In what ways does your life function to the world around you as a testimony of the "realness" of God?

DAY 3 LUKE 1:5-7

There are a couple of people who are really important to the Christmas story. They are really important to the overall story of Jesus and His life. And they may not be the two people you're thinking about.

Read Luke 1:5-7. Here you meet an older, married couple: Elizabeth and Zechariah. Zechariah was a priest, and a man tasked with representing his people before God in the Temple. He would have led them in worship and in making sacrifices and offerings. Elizabeth, his wife, was from the lineage of priests (that's the whole "from the daughter's of Aaron" line). In verse 6, we see that Elizabeth and Zechariah loved God and followed His ways. But in verse 7, we find an interesting contradiction.

In verse 7 we see that they had no child. When Luke's original audience read this verse after reading verses 5-6, they would have seen these two truths as contradictory. In Jewish culture, children were considered a blessing from God, and if you weren't able to have children, it was thought that God was judging you because of some sin in your life. Can you imagine how hard this must have been for them?

We tend to think that just because we're Christ-followers, things will go well for us. We ought to be happy. We ought to be free from struggle or strife. But that is rarely the case.

You see, in His grace, God journeys with us through hard times to grow our faith and our reliance on Him. It doesn't mean that He doesn't love us. It often means that He's preparing us for a blessing that will mean more because we waited on it.

CONSIDER THIS . . .

• What is something you wanted really badly that God didn't (or hasn't) choose to provide for you?

• Has enough time passed for you to look back and see why He decided not to give it to you? What lesson did you learn about God or yourself as a result?

• Zechariah and Elizabeth stayed faithful even though God had not yet granted their desires. What can you learn from their example?

DAY 4 LUKE 1:8-17

What is the best gift you have ever been given? Think about it. I'll wait.

Now that you've pictured this gift, do you remember what you felt like when you got it? Pretty amazing, right? Especially if it was a surprise. There is nothing quite like the feeling of getting a gift that you have wanted for some time. There's joy, thankfulness, and excitement all rolled into one experience.

Read Luke 1:8-17. So, stop for a moment and think about all those positive feelings you had when you got the new phone you always wanted, or the game system, or your first car. Think about those feelings and multiply them times a million. That had to be what Zechariah was feeling here.

You see, in the passage you just read, Zechariah found out he would be receiving the thing he and his wife had most longed for. In their old age, the couple would have a son. But this was not going to be any ordinary baby. This child, who would one day come to be known as John the Baptist, would help prepare the world for the coming of Jesus.

Throughout the Christmas story, we see these types of incredible interactions between God and His people. God was doing amazing things to make way for His Son, Jesus. Zechariah and Elizabeth had a small role to play. But what a remarkable story! As you think about their story, don't miss the application to your story. God is able and willing to work mightily through you to shake up the world for His glory. Pray to God and ask Him to use you in awesome ways, just like He used Zechariah, Elizabeth, and eventually, their son John.

CONSIDER THIS . . .

• Expecting God to work through you is part of God working through you. Do you expect God to use you? Why or why not?

• If you're expectant, you're ready. What role does being prepared for God to use you play in God actually using you?

• Take some time to pray today that God would open your eyes to the needs all around you. He is ready to work through you to impact the world for His name. Ask God to help make you willing to take action.

DAY 5 LUKE 1:18-25

Is there anything worse than people talking about you behind your back? OK, maybe it's worse when people are talking about you in front of your back. But the point is that it stinks when people gossip about us. Nobody likes to be dragged down. Especially if it's over something we didn't do.

When you find yourself the object of other people's gossip, you try your hardest to move on don't you? You try to act like it doesn't bother you. You try to be thick skinned and ignore the stares or the giggles or the veiled social media jabs. But deep down, it hurts.

Read Luke 1:18-25. Pay close attention to verses 24-25. When Elizabeth praised God for taking away her "reproach among people," she was talking about the very thing we were just talking about. She was talking about God removing the reason people all around her had talked about her behind her back.

In Elizabeth's culture, if you couldn't have a baby, it was seen as a sign of God's punishment for sin. So, Elizabeth would have carried around this shame her entire life, even though she had done nothing to deserve her infertility. But God miraculously removed her shame. And He did it for countless people in the New Testament. God is all about taking away the shame from our lives.

Wrapped up in the Christmas story is the story of Zechariah and Elizabeth. These were two ordinary people dealing with their issues. But God acted miraculously in their lives to both weave the big-picture story of His plan to send His Son to rescue the world, and to personally remove their pain and shame. This is what God does, time and time again. And if that doesn't remind us to awaken our sense of wonder about God and His work, I don't know what will.

CONSIDER THIS . . .

• How do you deal with relational issues that come up between you and your friends? What is God's role in it?

• Is there a burden in your life that you're carrying around that you haven't surrendered to God? What are you waiting for?

• Make it a point to spend some time in prayer, asking God to help you feel free of the shame of your brokenness. Ask Him to remind you of His great love for you, and His desire to forgive our sins.

DAY 6 LUKE 1:26-29

At the heart of the Christmas story is a young woman named Mary. As we make it a point to rediscover our sense of wonder about the Christmas story, let's look at Mary again with fresh eyes. Let's see what we can discover about her.

Read Luke 1:26-29. Here we learn that Mary is from Nazareth in Galilee. We're not the original audience, and so we miss the fact that Nazareth is a rinky-dink little town. Not exactly the place you'd expect to find the earthly mother of the Son of God. We also learn that Mary was a virgin engaged to be married to Joseph. In other words, she had never been with a man sexually. She was morally upright. She was also young. Most scholars believe Mary was only around 14 or 15 years old at the time. Mary was also highly confused.

Imagine yourself in Mary's shoes. You'd be confused too. One day Mary is just going about her everyday life, the next, an angel sent from the Lord was giving her a message. "Favored one"? What in the world was that all about? "A message from God to me"? Can you imagine how confused she must have been? Verse 29 says Mary was troubled and was trying to figure all of this out.

Relating to Mary is easy. While God may not choose to have you parent His Son, God does have plans for your life. Sometimes these plans may confuse you. If they do, don't worry. You're in good company. Mary was confused, too. But Mary ultimately trusted God's plan. That's your challenge today as well.

When God leads you down a road you're unsure of, know beyond a shadow of a doubt that it's precisely where you're supposed to be. Trust. Stay true. And keep your eyes open. You're God's plan to impact the world in His name.

CONSIDER THIS . . .

• Can you think of a time when you knew God was working in your life, but you didn't know exactly what He was doing? What emotions did you feel?

• If you aren't aware of God working in or through you, what does that say about your faith? (Here's a hint: God is always present and always at work. If you can't feel it, the issue is not with God.)

• Take a moment to pray today that God would help you have a clear vision to see what He is doing in your life.

DAY ⬛7 LUKE 1:30-33

You're reading this book at Christmas time. OK, do a little thought-exercise. Think ahead to the end of the school year. Do you remember what it's like to count down the final week before Summer? It's disturbing and exciting all at the same time. There is nothing quite like the days before you can walk away from school for the summer. The waiting is tough, but the reward is worth it.

Read Luke 1:30-33. For us to understand the news Mary received, we need a little background info. Sometime around a thousand years before Mary's time, King David ruled Israel. David was a good king and life in Israel was pretty good, for the most part. Then, David died, and his son Solomon was king. And things were still pretty great. But then, Solomon had to go and mess everything up.

Solomon turned away from God. And as a result, Israel would be split into two kingdoms after his death: a northern and a southern Kingdom. God sent the prophets to warn Israel to turn back to God. But they didn't listen. Within about 500 years, God allowed the destruction of both the northern and southern kingdoms. But all during this time, God continued to send a message of hope. He continued to promise that a Messiah would come. God promised to send His Son to be the hope of Israel and the world.

So you see, the Jews had been waiting for the Messiah for hundreds of years. Hundreds. And then one day, in a sleepy little town, an angel is telling Mary that the Messiah is here, and that she will be His mother. Can you even imagine what she must have felt like hearing the angel's words? Those words describe a powerful, miraculous ruler who would deliver people from their sins. Jesus would be the rescuer of the world. And He would be Mary's son. If that's not the most fantastic birth announcement ever written, I don't know what is.

CONSIDER THIS . . .

• Re-read verses 32-33. What description of Jesus most stands out to you?

• How has the good news of Jesus changed your life? Have you ever thought about the answer to that question?

• Is there someone in your life who needs to hear that Jesus is the king, come to redeem all people from their sins? What's keeping you from telling them?

We all have dreams. Some of those dreams are the "I can work hard enough and make this happen" sort of dream. Like making the team or club or attending your favorite college. Others are the "there is no way in the world I can pull this off, but it's fun to think about it" kind of dreams. You know, like wanting to be a TV star or a famous athlete. For the overwhelming majority of us, these are the kind of dreams that, no matter how badly we want them, they probably won't come true.

And while this is a major bummer, it's just the way it is. Some things aren't possible. Except when they are. Except when God gets involved.

Read Luke 1:34-38. Have you ever prayed for something you thought could never happen only to see it happen? Have you ever seen God "open a door" you thought was closed? Have you ever watched God blow away your human-based understanding with a God-sized movement?

Mary did. Mary watched God do the impossible. She watched Him defy the laws of nature. But before she saw the miracle, she had a moment where she doubted God. And while this isn't a good look for Mary, it helps us understand that she's human. She's just like us.

Look back at verse 34. For a moment, even face-to-face with an angel, Mary had an attack of humanity. "How can this happen?" Mary knew how babies were made, and she knew for a fact she wasn't a candidate! But Mary forgot one thing. The rules that she knew governed the creation of life? The process she was sure she had not been a part of? Mary forgot that God set those rules in place. God created the process! Thus, He can work outside the process when He chooses.

It sounds a little oversimplified, but it's true: Nothing is impossible with God.

CONSIDER THIS . . .

• Is your vision of God too small because you put limitations on Him? How might your relationship with God be different if you saw Him for who He was?

• Take a few minutes and praise God for His ability to keep our sense of wonder going strong. Ask for God to show you ways He has made the impossible "possible" in your life.

DAY 9 LUKE 1:38

We're going to spend one more day taking an in-depth look at Mary. After all, from the human side of things, she is one of the MAJOR players in the Christmas story. And so before you move on to the rest of the story, let's give Mary and her life one last long look.

Re-read Luke 1:38. In that moment, can you imagine what must have been going through Mary's mind? You're minding your business, doing whatever a 1st-century Jewish girl would have done on any given day. Maybe Mary was gathering firewood or fetching water. Perhaps she was sewing or cooking a meal. Whatever Mary was doing, it became unimportant, really quickly.

In the middle of what we can imagine might have been a typical day, an angel appeared. Let that sink in for a minute. You're Mary. You're doing what you do. And then, boom, Gabriel's in your living room! It's no wonder the first thing he said was basically, "Settle down! Don't freak out. We're cool!" We can only imagine how frightened we'd be if we were all of a sudden face-to-face with an angel.

But maybe the most unsettling thing was Gabriel's message. Imagine being told you were going to be pregnant. Keep in mind you're not married, so this message has its problems. Oh, and one more thing: the baby won't be your fiancé's. And it won't be conceived by human means. It will be God's child, His Son, the long-awaited Messiah, promised for centuries. How's that for an announcement?

Mary was confused. And rightfully so. It's crazy to think how hard it must have been to grasp a message like this. What would people say? Would they even believe her? What would Joseph think? And what did it mean that God's Son would live and grow inside her? The questions must have flooded Mary's mind.

But her response was pretty amazing. In verse 38, we see Mary do something powerful in its simplicity: she surrendered. "I'm the Lord's servant. I'm on board." Her obedience cleared the way for her to be one of the major players in the greatest story ever told.

CONSIDER THIS . . .

• Why is it so difficult to surrender our lives to God and allow Him to lead us?

• What does our hesitation say about our level of trust in God?

• Do you ever think about what God has planned for you that you miss out on because you want to be in control of your life instead of surrendering it to God?

Have you ever had your heart set on something only to be disappointed? I know I have. When you don't get the thing you want, or it doesn't go your way, there's always this moment of letdown. You are stuck dealing with the emotions you feel when the thing you want slips out of your grasp. In the aftermath of not getting something I wanted, a large part of why I feel the way I do is tied up in my expectations. If I can adjust my expectations, I usually deal with disappointment pretty well. But if I have REALLY been counting on something, it's tough for me to move on. Can you relate?

Read Matthew 1:18-25. Joseph found himself dealing with some pretty mixed up expectations. What he expected was that his engagement would go smoothly, and he would marry his sweetheart. And yet, Joseph was met with some news that must have crushed him: Mary was pregnant. Not only that, but she claimed it was God who had conceived the baby inside of her. As we'll look at more closely tomorrow, Joseph ultimately made the right call. He eventually believed Mary. All was well. But do you ever wonder if he still struggled a bit with unmet expectations?

Sure, Joseph was an awesome, amazing part of God's plan to rescue humankind from their sins. But do you ever wonder how Joseph felt about this? Maybe he was shy and simple. Perhaps he didn't want the pressure of being part of God's plan. His expectations of a "normal" marriage went away pretty quickly. But to Joseph's credit, he rolled with it. He adjusted his expectations, got used to his "new normal," and devoted himself to Mary and Jesus.

God will often do things differently than we want or expect. We can let this derail us, or, we can trust God and go with His flow. We know what Joseph chose. What would you choose?

CONSIDER THIS . . .

• Think of a time when God did something for you or through that was awesome, but that completely went against your expectations. How did it make you feel?

• How can our expectations sometimes be an excuse to do things the same old way we've always done them?

• Are you brave enough to pray and ask God to blow away your expectations of Him and how He wants to use you?

DAY ▋▋ MATTHEW 1:24-25

Think of a time when someone told you something you didn't believe. They swore it was true. But for whatever reason, you couldn't bring yourself to believe him or her. Maybe you were on the other end. Have you ever tried to convince someone of something only to be told you weren't telling the truth?

Read Matthew 1:24-25. Think about Joseph. Joseph and Mary were to be married, but Mary "was found to be with child." Now, Matthew lets us know that it was the Holy Spirit's work. But, look at Joseph's response: He was going to break off the marriage.

Apparently, Mary told Joseph about the angel, but for whatever reason, Joseph didn't seem willing to believe her. (Or maybe he did, but was unwilling to face the ridicule of his friends and neighbors.) Matthew tells us that Joseph was a good man. But who could have blamed him for wanting out of the marriage? Imagine if your fiancé told you she was pregnant with God's baby. Would you be quick to believe her?

Thankfully, God wasn't done with Joseph. He sent an angel to tell Joseph that Mary was telling the truth. It must have been bittersweet for Joseph. He must have felt excited to learn what was happening, but maybe a twinge of shame that he didn't stick with Mary in the first place.

The coolest thing about Joseph? His willingness to trust that God would make it all work out. Joseph heard the angel's message and essentially said, "OK. I'm in. I don't understand all this, but I'll trust God." As Christ-followers, we're called to have the same trust in God. We might not always understand where God is leading us. But like Joseph, we can trust that God is in control. He knows where He's taking us. And that's all that matters.

CONSIDER THIS . . .

• Do you know precisely what God has in store for you in the near future? What college you'll attend? Who you'll marry, etc.? (Of course not.)

• How does trust in God help you navigate the many decisions about your future you're facing or will be facing soon?

• What does your level of trust in God say about how well you know Him? What can you do to grow on your faith in God?

DAY 12 LUKE 1:39-45

When cool things happen to us, it's only natural that we share the good news. Think of how weird it would be for you to have something genuinely amazing happen to you, and you told no one. No texting your friends. No posting about it on Instagram. Nothing. This situation isn't likely to happen, is it? Good news seems better when we have someone to share it with.

If you have a second, think of a particularly exciting event you've recently experienced. Write it down on the left side of the space below. Then, on the right side, write down the first three people you told.

Take a moment and read Luke 1:39-45. Just like you went and shared your exciting news with the people you listed above, Mary couldn't wait to tell her cousin Elizabeth of the news. Whether Mary knew of Elizabeth's news or not, we don't know for sure. But the cool thing is that BOTH women had exciting news to share. The coolest thing of all is that Elizabeth's excitement bubbled over in a Holy Spirit-fueled burst of joy that affirmed the angel's message to Mary: the baby in Mary's stomach was indeed the Messiah, God's Son.

Part of the idea of rediscovering our sense of wonder for the truths of the Christmas story is to apply its teachings to your own life. Would you say that you are still excited about the work God is doing in and through you? Or have you lost your sense of wonder when it comes to your faith? God IS working in you. Every day. And He is working through you, to reach the world in His name. Don't fall into the trap of getting so used to this fact that you take it for granted. Take a tip from Mary and Elizabeth. Embrace the wonder and excitement for what God is doing.

CONSIDER THIS . . .

• What obstacles keep you from being more aware of the work God is doing in your life?

• What can you do to minimize these obstacles, and make room for more excitement about what God is doing?

• Spend a few moments in prayer to God, thanking Him for all He continues to do in and through you and asking Him to help lead you to a place where you can express joy and excitement over His role in your life.

Here's a fun question: What in your life brings you joy? Is it a possession, like your car or a guitar? Is it something a bit more meaningful like your family? Maybe it's a hobby. Maybe cheerleading or football or band makes you happy. Many things in our lives bring us joy. Some of them we think about often (like family or friends). Some of them we may kind of take for granted (like food, or our health).

Read Luke 1:46-56. Mary wasn't about to take anything for granted. Again, she had just had a pretty amazing interaction. So, she headed over to see her cousin, Elizabeth. Elizabeth had some pretty cool news of her own: she was pregnant with her first child when most women her age were raising grandkids. (Elizabeth would give birth to John the Baptist.) When Mary and Elizabeth saw each other and shared their news, Mary burst into a meaningful song of thankfulness.

One of the truths about our relationship with God is that He is our provider. He is the giver of good things. He is the source of all our blessings: our health, our life, our shelter, our food, and so on. Sure, God might not literally pay your family's mortgage each month or put gas in your car. But the money your family earns? The job your mom or dad has? Maybe even the job you have? It's yours through God's grace. All good things come from God.

Mary seemed to have a firm grasp on this. Do you? Are you in the habit of realizing what God has given you and then making sure He hears your thankfulness? It starts with stepping back and seeing that God has given you more than you could ever imagine. When you understand this, praise and thankfulness come naturally.

CONSIDER THIS . . .

• List out your blessings. Think of everything good in your life and write them down. (Or at least write a few of them.)

• Now, stop and thank God for giving you all of these things.

• Why do you think an awareness of what you have and an attitude of thankfulness is so vital to a healthy relationship with God?

Take a moment and read John 1:57-62. Elizabeth is old, way past her child-birthing years. We've already talked about what it means to her reputation that God has decided to bless her in this way. It is a real miracle. And when we look at verse 58, people's reactions reflect this. People are pumped and are praising God as a result of this miraculous new thing that has happened. But then, we watch as their reaction changes a bit.

Tension enters the narrative at verse 59. When Elizabeth goes to name the boy John, just as the angel had instructed her, people freak out. The people turn to what they know best: tradition and custom. They essentially said, "Whoa, whoa, whoa! You don't have anyone in your family named John. Why not name him after his dad?" And not bothering to even listen to Elizabeth, they go to chat with Zechariah about it. I guess they thought he'd be the kind of guy to uphold tradition.

Now, read verses 62-66 (remember that Zechariah has been unable to talk for months, due to his initial disbelief that God would bless him with a son). It's hilarious that all the folks who were like, "that's not the way we do it around here" got put in their place. Zechariah supported Elizabeth, and God, and told the people the boy would DEFINITELY be called John. His boldness was backed up with God giving him his voice back. The people had to know something new and amazing was happening. It shattered their understanding of "it's just how things are done."

Sometimes the "way things have always been" is what keeps us from experiencing a sense of wonder about what God is doing. The key to still being in awe about God is to continue to look for God to be God. Enlarge your expectations. Don't box God in. Don't try to make Him fit your human-sized perspective. Look for God to do massive, awesome, amazing things. And get ready to join the work He is already doing.

CONSIDER THIS . . .

• Do you try to make God safe and predictable? Do you try to box Him in? If so, why?

• While we can know God, which is a beautiful thing, we'll never fully understand Him. His ways are too profound and grand for us. This is actually an awesome thing. Why?

• Say a prayer and ask God to help you see through any old customs or traditions keeping you from pursuing Him more.

DAY  15 LUKE 1:67-80

Today we take our last look at Zechariah and Elizabeth. You may wonder why they play such an essential role in the Christmas story. That's a fair question. First, it's impossible to separate John the Baptist's ministry from Jesus' ministry. John was part of God's plan from day 1. John's birth story is directly tied to Jesus' birth story. But there is another reason we celebrate Zechariah and Elizabeth as part of the Christmas narrative.

Read Luke 1:67-80. This is the continuation of the story you started yesterday. This is Zechariah's response after seeing God keep His promise of a son. (Keep in mind, these would have been the first real words that came out of Zechariah's mouth for months!) And in his response, we see why he has such an important role in the Christmas story.

What do you see in Zechariah's words here? In verses 68-75, Zechariah is giving us a super-quick overview of God's covenant promises made to His people throughout the Old Testament. Zechariah is combining what he knows about Jesus' birth to Mary and Joseph, with what he has been told about his son John's life. He is putting the pieces together and realizing that something HUGE is happening. He is seeing God working as only God can. Zechariah knows something special is about to go down.

Verses 68-69 say, "Blessed be the Lord God of Israel, for he has visited and redeemed his people and has raised up a horn of salvation for us in the house of his servant David." This is what Christmas is all about. This is what we celebrate! In Christ, God visited us. In Jesus, God raised up a path to salvation. Through Jesus' death on the cross, we can be redeemed from the penalty of our sins. And it all started with a little God-baby born in humble surroundings. This is the miracle of Christmas! This is Immanuel!

CONSIDER THIS . . .

• In your own words, summarize the meaning of Christmas.

• Why is it easy to miss the meaning of Christmas as we go through this busy holiday season?

• What can you do to make sure that you don't lose sight of what Christmas is truly about?

DAY 16 LUKE 2:1-7

What does it mean to be confident? To be confident means expecting an outcome and acting on it accordingly. Confidence is jumping out of a plane believing the thin piece of silk in your backpack will stop your fall. Confidence is walking across a crosswalk believing cars will stop at a red light. Confidence is going to sleep at night believing the world will be as it should be when you wake up.

Read Luke 2:1-7. While it might not seem at first like the most obvious concept, confidence actually plays a pretty prominent role in the passage you just read.

Where do we see it? Verse 6. Time had passed since God's revelation to Mary and Joseph. And here they were traveling to Bethlehem to be counted in the Roman census. What would happen? What would God do? Would God do as He promised? Was there another surprise in store?

Confidence was a gift given to Mary and Joseph in the form of a baby, born just as God said He would be. Fully God, the Messiah that would take away the sins of the world. Fully human, the little baby wrapped in clothes, lying in a feeding trough. God came through. Because of this, Mary and Joseph could have confidence that God was who He said He was and would accomplish what He said He would accomplish.

Confidence. It's believing that God can and will do what He says He will do. It's taking His promises in the Bible as truth. It's living your life in a bold, vibrant faith knowing that God will use you to grow His Kingdom.

Confidence. Do you have it?

CONSIDER THIS . . .

• What has God done in your life to build your confidence in Him?

• There is a lot of uncertainty in the world these days. How does confidence in God's character affect any fears or worries you have in your life?

DAY 17 COLOSSIANS 1:15-20

Turn in your Bible or your Bible app to Colossians 1:15-20. You've just read the part in the story where Jesus was born, and you're just a few days away from celebrating His birth with Christ-followers around the world. Let's take this moment to look a little more closely at precisely whom it was that was born in that manger.

Read Colossians 1:15-20. This is one of the most amazing descriptions of Jesus in the Bible. Paul says that Jesus is "the image of the invisible God." When we "see" Jesus in the Bible, we see God in human form. Paul said Jesus was "the firstborn of all creation." Jesus, the same little boy, born in a manger, is the Prince of all created things. Paul says in verse 16, "For by him all things were created, in heaven and on earth, visible and invisible, whether thrones or dominions or rulers or authorities." The baby born to Mary and Joseph that night was with God when the earth was spoken into being. Paul writes that "all things were created through him and for him." Jesus was the author and the object of Creation. The world exists to glorify Him. In verse 17 Paul says, "And he is before all things, and in him all things hold together." The same Jesus that spent His first night in a meager stable is the unifying force that keeps all of creation moving forward.

The frail newborn looking up at Mary and Joseph? Paul wrote that He is "the head of the body, the church. He is the beginning, the firstborn from the dead, that in everything he might be preeminent." This seemingly normal looking baby whose birth angels foretold? "In him all the fullness of God was pleased to dwell."

Most importantly, the God-child we celebrate on Christmas would be the lynchpin of God's plan to rescue humanity from sin and death. Through Jesus, God would "reconcile to himself all things, whether on earth or in heaven, making peace by the blood of his cross."

This is the baby we celebrate! Jesus is the culmination of God's plan to redeem humankind from the separation sin causes. And maybe the most amazing thing about it all is that this very Jesus knows you, and chooses to let you know Him.

CONSIDER THIS . . .

• Take some time today and PRAISE Jesus for who He is. Praise Him for His identity, but also for who He is to you personally.

DAY 18 LUKE 2:8-14

Have you ever been in a situation where suddenly your assumptions or thoughts about a specific person or thing were pretty much blown off the map? Maybe it was the moment you realized the little test you were "prepared" for was really an overwhelming obstacle you had no chance of conquering. Or the moment you realized that she really does like you, a lot! Or how about the moment you realized your team is completely overmatched. Or . . . Well, you get the point. There are moments of clarity where what you thought was the case may not necessarily be the case at all.

Read Luke 2:8-14. The shepherds who were in the fields outside of Bethlehem? They experienced one of those moments in a big, big way.

It's safe to say that the shepherds knew God. Or they knew of Him as well as they could. They were Israelites. Their people had a rich history with God. They were, after all, God's people. But, everything they thought they knew about God and His ways were pretty much overwhelmed that night. All of a sudden, the God who was a little distant and a lot mysterious, was right up in their world. In their faces!

Look at the description in verse 9: "the glory of the Lord shone around them." Can you imagine? God was no longer an idea. He was real. He had broken the invisible barrier between His Kingdom and this world. And it's entirely safe to say the world was never the same.

Isn't that a pretty good way to think about the Christmas story in general? Isn't it as simple as God breaking the barrier and coming into our world? That's what "Immanuel" is all about, isn't it? God literally with us? It is that simple. Yet, the power behind this simple truth is life changing.

You are who you are today because God chose to send His Son into this world.

CONSIDER THIS . . .

• Answer this: How does Christ coming into our world change things? What would your relationship with God be like if God had not designed it this way?

• Consider thanking God for His love that compelled Him to send Jesus into our world.

DAY 19 LUKE 2:15-21

Read Luke 2:15-21. The shepherds saw something they weren't expecting. Their sense of wonder was awakened and set in high gear! They had an encounter with God's Kingdom in a fantastic way. Afterward, they were left with a choice.

What were they to do with the information they just heard?

The truth is that once we encounter Christ, each of us, you included, has a choice to make. When people hear the Gospel or have a chance to encounter Christ through the Bible, there is a choice to be made. People have to respond one way or another. They will either move on this information, or they will not. They will either be compelled to know more, or the will choose to walk away.

The shepherds had a choice. They made their choice, and they made it well.

The shepherds acted, and they retold. They acted on the angels' message. Look in verse 15. They heard, and they moved. They could have sat and talked, or they could have gone home. But they didn't. They followed through, and they were rewarded by coming face-to-face with the Son of God.

But they didn't stop with merely acting. They retold. Verse 17 says that once they were sure of the angels' message, they couldn't contain themselves. They started talking. They started spreading the word about Jesus. It was as if they couldn't keep quiet.

Today, over two thousand years later, we're still expected to do the same. If you know Christ, you should find yourself compelled to speak of His story. If you have encountered God and His Kingdom, you know that you will find it hard to keep your mouth shut.

You have to move. You have to act. And with God empowering you, you will. And you'll be awesome.

CONSIDER THIS . . .

• What's keeping you from being a more powerful teller of Jesus' story? What can you do to be more committed to being someone who tells Jesus' story to others?

DAY 20 LUKE 2:8-20

We know it all. We've seen it all. It's tough to slip something past us we haven't heard of before. While this isn't exactly true, we've been conditioned to feel like it is. With the prevalence of information at our fingertips, it certainly feels like just about everything worth knowing is available to be known.

And when we do see something we haven't seen before, we tend not to believe it's real. When every celebrity is Photoshopped to perfection, and when every movie is CGI'd to the point where we don't know what's real and what isn't, who can blame us?

You might say we've lost our sense of wonder. And that's a bad thing. Wonder is like curiosity times ten. It's the spirit of discovery. It's looking at the world around us with a healthy dose of "I can still be impressed, surprised, or amazed."

Read Luke 2:8-20. The shepherds had a huge sense of wonder. They had just witnessed a holy concert, a heavenly performance unlike any ever heard. And they were amazed. Moved by this, they took off running, acting on their strong sense of wonder, heading out to discover if what they had been told was true.

And of course, they found that it was true. As true as anything could ever be. Their wonder was rewarded. They were amazed. Moved. Transfixed. All because they possessed an amazing curiosity and openness about God and His ways.

How is your sense of wonder?

CONSIDER THIS . . .

• What was the last thing, whether it was an experience or something you learned, that stopped you in your tracks and made you say, "wow"?

• Why is it so easy to go through the motions of life, failing to have any wonder about the world around you?

• Can you know all there is to know about God? (Hint: no) What role does wonder play in knowing God better?

DAY 21 MATTHEW 2:1-6

If you think about it, we can define significant moments in our lives by how we respond to them. When a problem arises, it's often not the problem itself that impacts us. It's the way in which we respond to it. When an opportunity presents itself, the difference is whether or not you respond by seizing it, or by letting it pass you by. When we look back at many situations in life, our response can either be seen as right or wrong.

Now, read Matthew 2:1-6. Here is the familiar story of the wise men. Now, you know this story. (But did you know that biblical scholars believe that the wise men came to visit Jesus several months (some say even years) after He was born?) But I want you to look at it with fresh eyes. I want you to look at it with this concept of "reactions" in mind.

If you had to describe the wise men's reaction to Jesus, what words would you use? Curious? Inquisitive? Seeking? However you describe it, the point is that the wise men saw something in the stars that they regularly studied, and rightly interpreted it as a sign that something spectacular has happened. Their response was the right one: they sought out Jesus, the King of the Jews.

But look at Herod's response. How would you describe it? Calculated? Fearful? Power-hungry? Psychotic? Herod, the Roman-appointed ruler over this region, was a tyrant. And instead of being curious about the spiritual implications of Jesus' birth, Herod's response was wrong. He was scared that his power would be threatened. He was fearful who Jesus might be.

People still respond to Jesus in one of these two ways. They are either curious about who Jesus is and what He can do in and through them, or they are dismissive, fearful, or downright apathetic. Your life is a billboard for Jesus. The way you live tells the world that you belong to Christ. People will respond to Jesus in you. And their response will either be right, or wrong.

CONSIDER THIS . . .

• Are you responsible for how people respond to Jesus? What ARE you responsible for?

• How do you communicate the Gospel to the world around you? What are some examples of how you do this in your words? What are some examples of how you do this through your actions?

What is worship? If you immediately thought about singing, don't worry: that IS worship. But worship is way more than just praising God in song. Worship is one of those concepts we know when we see it, but that can sometimes be hard to put it into words. I want to give you a definition of worship, one that builds on our discussion from yesterday about responses. You ready for the definition? Worship is a right reaction to an encounter with God.

Let's break this down a bit. First, think about when you encounter God. You can encounter God in the Bible, in nature, through prayer, by the conviction of the Holy Spirit, even through Christian community. Worship is simply how you respond to God once you recognize that you've encountered Him. Now do you see why worship is bigger than singing praise songs in church?

Read Matthew 2:7-12. The wise men didn't know exactly whom they would meet when they encountered Jesus. At least we don't think so. Based on the Bible, we know they expected to meet "the King of the Jews." But I am willing to bet they were surprised when they saw a young child in meager surroundings. Whether they were surprised or not, we can't say. But we can say this: when they encountered Jesus, the responded rightly. In other words, they worshipped! They gave Jesus the glory and honor He was due.

Let me ask you this: as you go throughout this Christmas season, are you looking for encounters with God? Are you expecting to encounter Him? Are you seeking places to sense His presence or see the works of His hand? You know, so much about our faith hinges on the idea of expectancy. We get too busy, especially this time of year. And we don't EXPECT to encounter God. When you do finally slow down enough to realize you're encountering God, be sure to focus on your response. Make sure you respond rightly, with worship to God for all He is and for all He has done. That's the best way to re-focus on God this Christmas season.

CONSIDER THIS . . .

• Today, be more aware of where you may encounter God. Look for Him in the Bible, through prayer, in the world around you . . . look for Him expecting to meet Him. And then respond with real, authentic worship.

DAY 23 LUKE 2:22-32

Who is the most rock-solid person in your life? You know the one: that person who is with you through thick and thin. The one who was there when no one else was. For many of you, it is a parent or grandparent. For others, it may be your best friend from school or church. No matter who it is, faithful friends are priceless. There aren't many blessings in this world better than someone who doesn't give up or give in.

As we get ready to wrap up this time of focusing on the true meaning of the Christmas story, maybe it's good that we finish with this passage from Luke 2:22-32. Because this passage is all about faithfulness. It's all about not giving up or flaking out.

First, let's look at the faithfulness of Mary and Joseph. In this passage, we see them being faithful to the spiritual traditions of their people, the Jews. But more than this, Mary and Joseph have proven faithful throughout the entire story of Jesus' birth. They never wavered. And look at the faithfulness of Simeon! Simeon served day-in and day-out, waiting for the Lord to send a Savior. He never gave up. And he eventually had his faithfulness rewarded. Finally, God proved faithful in a variety of ways. He came through with His promise of a Messiah. And He was faithful in rewarding Simeon's service. Faithfulness is all over this story!

Faithfulness is one of the best qualities we can have. We model God when we demonstrate faithfulness. God is perfectly faithful in all His ways. And our call is to be faithful to Him. It's tempting to view our relationship with God as something we turn on or off depending on our surroundings. But faith doesn't work this way. Even though the road may be hard, we have to stay true to our faith in God. After all, God is true to us in every way. It's the least we can do in return.

CONSIDER THIS . . .

- During this Christmas season, how have you seen your faith in God grow? Moving forward, what are some areas in your life where you could be more faithful in your commitment to follow Jesus?
- Say a prayer today asking God to remind you what it means to be faithful, and to give you the strength to follow through.

DAY 24 — LUKE 2:7

"And she gave birth to her firstborn son and wrapped him in swaddling cloths and laid him in a manger, because there was no place for them in the inn." - Luke 2:7

Let your imagination run wild for a bit.

Can you imagine what that night must have been like 2,000 or so years ago? Imagine Mary, nine months pregnant, riding on a donkey trying to find a place to stay the night. She had to know her delivery was close. Imagine the sounds and the smells of the stable in which she and Joseph finally hunkered down. And imagine what it must have been like to give birth to a baby. In a barn.

What do you think was going through Mary and Joseph's minds? It's impossible to know for sure. But it's safe to say they were probably thankful, exhausted, relieved . . . and maybe a little bit in awe. God had done what He said He would do. He promised a baby, and here he was.

I wonder if when Mary held baby Jesus' hands, she had any idea how those hands would pay the price for the sins of the entire world. I wonder if she dreamed of the fame and glory He would find on this earth? Do you think she had any inkling how He would suffer for our sake?

We know the entire story. We have a benefit Mary and Joseph didn't have on that night. We can see those events in light of the rest of the story. But on that night, all Mary and Joseph knew was that God had sent His Son to be their son. And He had arrived. Safe and sound.

Tonight, as you read this, put yourself in that stable in Bethlehem so many years ago. Think about what it must have been like. Use your imagination. And prepare your heart to celebrate Jesus' birth.

CONSIDER THIS . . .

• Today, be more aware of where you may encounter God. Look for Him in the Bible, through prayer, in the world around you . . . look for Him expecting to meet Him. And then respond with real, authentic worship.

DAY 24 CHRISTMAS EVE
FAMILY DEVOTION

As a family, read the entire Christmas narrative as it's told in Luke.

FIRST, take turns reading from Luke 1:5 – Luke 2:21.

THEN, when you've finished, go around the room and take turns sharing which parts of the story stand out as significant to you.

NEXT, take a moment and answer this question:

I am thankful God sent Jesus to this earth because _____.

FINALLY, considering wrapping up your time of devotion by singing your favorite Christmas song(s) together as a family. Close in a prayer thanking God for loving us enough to send His Son to save us from our sins.

What a wonderful day to celebrate the birth of our Savior. With Jesus' birth comes hope, joy, and peace for all humankind.

This is a day to spend enjoying time with family and reflecting on all that Christmas means to you. But before you do, read Isaiah 9:2-7 paying close attention to verses 6 and 7. You've read them before. They are familiar. But on this day, let their words sink in.

Wonderful Counselor. Mighty God. Everlasting Father. Prince of Peace.

Jesus is all of these things. And today is a day to celebrate God's decision to send Him into our world.

Enjoy this beautiful day with your friends and family.

DAY 25 CHRISTMAS DAY
FAMILY DEVOTION

Here's a short devotional thought for you and your family on Christmas day.

FIRST, look at your Christmas tree. Have each person find an ornament that represents an aspect of the Christmas narrative. You may have some ornaments that are obvious connections to the Christmas story: stars, a manger, maybe even miniature nativity scenes. But it doesn't have to be literal. For instance, you might find an ornament of a toy; for you, it may represent the wise men giving Jesus gifts. Or maybe it's a cross ornament; this could represent Jesus and His birth. Whatever the case, take a moment and let each family member find an ornament that represents an aspect of the Christmas story.

THEN, take a moment for each person to share why they picked what they did.

FINALLY, when you've finished, have someone say a prayer for the family. Thank God for the gift of Christmas and all that it represents.

ABOUT THE AUTHOR
ANDY BLANKS

Andy Blanks is the Publisher and Co-Founder of YM360. A former Marine, he has worked in worked in youth ministry, mostly in the field of publishing, for nearly 15 years. During that time, Andy has led the development of some of the most popular Bible study curriculum and discipleship resources in the country. He has authored numerous books, Bible studies, and articles, and regularly speaks at events and conferences, both for adults and teenagers. But Andy's passion is communicating the transforming truth of the God's Word, which he does in his local church on a weekly basis.

Andy and his wife, Brendt, were married in 2000. They have four children, three girls and one boy.

MEET YOUTH MINISTRY'S MOST USED STUDENT DEVOTIONALS

THE DISCIPLESHIP BUNDLE FROM YM360 PROVIDES THREE POWERFUL, 4-WEEK DEVOTIONAL EXPERIENCES TO HELP YOU GROW INTO AUTHENTIC DISCIPLES OF JESUS

NEW: First Steps For Christ-Followers is a powerful experiential journal which will help students take the first steps on their new journey with Christ.

NEXT: Growing A Faith That Lasts helps challenge and equip you to take ownership of your faith.

NOW: Impacting Your World For Christ (Right Now!) will help you understand the purpose God has in store for you; catch God's VISION for exactly how He wants to use you; and practice real ways to impact your world.

FOR SAMPLES OR FOR ORDERING INFO, SIMPLY GO TO

YM360.COM/DEVOBUNDLE